Hope Restoring

Hope Restoring: Modern Day Psalms to Comfort and Inspire

Volume One in the Grace Lane Poetry collection
Published in 2023 by Dawnlight Publishing

ISBN 978-1-99-116982-2 (paperback)
ISBN 978-1-99-117684-4 (hardcover)

Text © Kataleya Graceal 2023
Book design © Dream Co Media
The moral right of the author has been asserted.
Sketch artwork by Mary Marinan

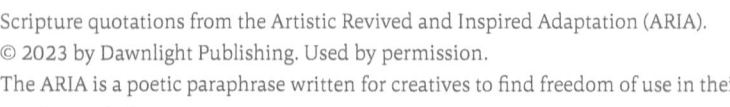

Scripture quotations from the Artistic Revived and Inspired Adaptation (ARIA).
© 2023 by Dawnlight Publishing. Used by permission.
The ARIA is a poetic paraphrase written for creatives to find freedom of use in their creative projects.

Scripture quotation from the King James Version (KVJ) ~ public domain use.

A catalogue record for this book is available from the National Library of New Zealand

All rights reserved. No part of this publication may be reproduced, stored in a retrieval system, or transmitted, in any form or by any means, electronic, mechanical, photocopying, recording or otherwise, without the prior written permission of the publisher. The only exception is brief quotations for the purpose of printed reviews.
This book is sold subject to the condition that it shall not, by way of trade or otherwise, be lent, re-sold, hired out or otherwise circulated without the publisher's prior consent in any form of binding or cover other than that in which it is published and without similar condition including this condition being imposed on the subsequent purchaser.

Hope Restoring

MODERN DAY PSALMS
TO COMFORT AND INSPIRE

Poetic inspiration
by Kataleya Graceal

Sketch artwork
by Mary Marinan

Contents

Reveal	8
Soul Food	9
Shepherd in the Storm	11
Warm Hope	12
A Loud Whisper	13
Warmth	14
Love in Heart	15
Keeping My Head Above Water	16
Like	17
My Aid	18
A Prayer of Thanksgiving	21
With You	22
Kind Eyes	23
Awakening	24
Thank You	26
Today's Treasures	27
Saving Grace	28
Rain/Reign	30
Trusting	33

Gone	35
Joy Full	36
Revival	37
By	38
Bottled Tears	40
Warm Arms	42
In All	43
Victory	44
Hope	47
Look Up	48
Free	50
Light	52
Praise	53
Dance of Life	54
Shining	57
Knowing (the Unseen Realm)	58
Light and Free	61
Like Honey	62
Transcending	63
Delight	64

The Lord is my Shepherd,
so I won't be in want or lack
anything I need.

He gives me rest so I can
stretch out in lush, sun-
filled green meadows, and
He leads me beside calm,
peaceful waters.

Psalm 23: 1-2 ARIA

Reveal

Seeking

    the One to be sought.

Your face,

    not just hands

        Truth,

            not darkness.

        Seek

            reveal

                find.

Seek the Lord and His strength; continually seek His face forever.
Psalm 105:4 NKJV

Soul Food
A prayer of thanksgiving

What feeds us?

What fuels us?

Is it the Bread of Life?

I come to You today,

As I ponder away –

a daily uplifting of my eyes,

and sit and receive.

To give You thanks, God,

for all You provide –

deep, nourishing, inner food

that's well for my body

and well for my soul.

Shepherd in the Storm

A prayer in need,
a friend in need
> Oh that You would come
> and be beside us in the storm.

I clasp my hands
with a friend of old
> In desperation we cry out
> that the dust will turn to gold.

Who are You? we ponder and say
> To say who You are melts our tears away

Mighty, Counsellor,
Shepherd in the storm,
Almighty, Powerful,
> Healer to all, warm.

Warm Hope

'Oh little one, so precious to Me,
Hope is coming, it'll come,
and it'll be.
Hope is uncovering the darkness;
a shimmering light
a beam of light
contains no evil
Hope is My hope,
a warmth that remains.'

A Loud Whisper

A whisper in the night,
    please help,
like a loud shout in the day.
Oh, the many tears in our hearts.
Please help us, God.
Oh, please help us.
    My voice trembles.
But Your voice makes enemies tremble,
    like the roar of crashing ocean waves,
the roar of power
    that can wash away my pain.
Please take hold of my voice,
    as I give You my trembling prayers,
to become as bold as a lion,
that's now very aware.
    In Your strength I need not shake.
Instead, stand up and gird up
    and rest in Your wake
    safe, under Your feathered covering.

Warmth

Dear God,

Real warmth

deeper layer

a hug

an embrace in everlasting arms

a smile in Your eyes

that tells a thousand psalms

Your warming presence,

I'm thankful for.

Love in Heart

A gentle breeze blows across my shoulders,
warmth from the sun alights upon my face
As I turn towards it
a smile that is full of love
meets my eyes,
the eyes of Your heart.

Keeping My Head Above Water

Keeping me sane,
keeping me alive.

God, I thank you
for keeping me safe.
I pray,
please continue to
do so.

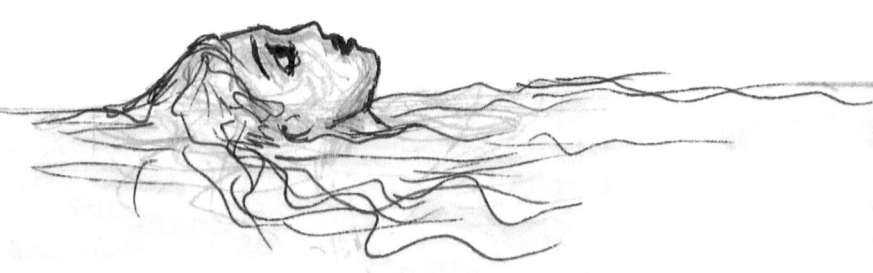

Like

Like raindrops dancing on my fingertips

    as I look up to the sky and see abundance

      falling

        like…

My Aid

Lord,
    please act quickly,
        please come to my aid!

I know who You are,
Father of Fathers
    and I will not let an enemy tell me otherwise,
    that You're truly the Lord of Hosts
        ready and able.

I come into Your arms
    where my prayers once hard to say,
      are now melting
        like warmth assurances of promises
          no longer stilted.

You are who You are,
        and I'm thankful to be Your child
    as the apple of Your eye,

You who protect and provide
        Who cares and decides,
    that life's going to be good,
      so no more hiding,
          I'm lifting my hood.

For I know the thoughts that I think toward you, saith the Lord, thoughts of peace, and not of evil.

Jeremiah 29:11 KJV

...this time
like a light in a dark room.
The dark fleeing away...
Remembering no more.

Once more I was brought to my knees.
I cried out.
But this time it was
my heart
in a swell of...
calling that You have moved before.
Something that was closed,
now open — a door.
I forget Your everything...
remember how

A Prayer of Thanksgiving

There was a time
> like a light in a dark room
> The dark fleeing away...
>> Remembering no more

Once more I was brought to my knees
  as I cried out.
> But this time it was with a
>> heart of joy,
> in a swell of gratitude,

recalling that You have moved before.
> Something that was closed,
>> now open – a door.
> How could I forget Your everything...

Now I'm grateful to remember how
> amazing You are, and grateful to
>> say thank You once more.

With You

By the seaside I rest,
    and spend time with You
Where to pray?
    Oh, here is where I'd like to stay
        Oh, here is where I'd like to say,
Thank You for making a beautiful world,
    nature, animals
        green spaces, oceans galore.
I pray for that those who've not yet found You
    that they would remember the pain of
    destruction on this earth
        no more.
But instead have hope,
    open eyes
        to see beauty that surrounds us
with a smile
    I pray that they would see beyond the sea,
        the horizon
    and capture *Your* heart
        smiling at them,
            for them, forever.

Kind Eyes

Oh how I long

    to just be where You are.

        To see You…

Those eyes – I know are kind.

Gazing

    finding….

        help

            strength

                assurance,

        knowing You're here.

Awakening

Drowning in the depths of despair
Thrashing, gulping in deep water;
do I just let go...
Will You help me, God?
I ask in a deep breath

Do I trust?
or let the waters overwhelm,
completely...
You hear our hearts,
I know You know,
I take one more breath...
and although I can't see it yet
I can feel the darkness shifting
You who is Always
won't let me stay here,
in this I trust.

'He sent help from the heavens, taking hold of me and rescuing me out of deep, turbulent waters.'
                    Psalm 18:16 ARTA

Thank You

Oh Lord,
> we come to You in thanks.

Thank You for who You are
> what You give

Who we are made to be
> opportunities aplenty

A way in the wilderness
> that You love and You care for us

For Your saving light
> Your truthful sword

That way of life
> the Gift You've shown us
>> Thank You.

Today's Treasures

One day. Oh, Lord, I'm dreaming of *one day...*
    But today is today
        and there could be treasure in this day.

There could be treasure to find,
if one just looks around
at what God might want to do
in this beautiful day,
    today.

Your Word guides us to think only of today,
    'Not to worry about tomorrow dear little ones,'
    I hear You say.

The sun rises and sets,
        bringing new as days reset
The moon has its time too
    As sleep sets in, to heal and dream
    and to take stock, being thankful
    for all the good things
        You've provided in today.

Saving Grace

Oh those waves that are still crashing.
                                      I can't breathe,
    swallowing undrinkable water

Amazing Savior, I cry out to you –
        Jesus…
        send Your saving hand
        to reach, lift me up,
        lift me out –
                so I can catch a breath.

        A light,
        a break, the water
                turning white –

For there are no words ready, that You, O Lord don't already know what I'm about to say. If I'm taken by the wings of dawn and dwell in the deepest parts of the sea, even there.

To see Your saving grace
      a light in the midst of dark waters
            now an arm wrapped around
    my waist.

  Yet,
        I now see Your saving arm was
            already there

As I surface,
   catch air in my lungs
      think of things lovely
        things above,
I can't help but think of how thankful
     I am to You for saving me.

I'll know Your hand leads me and Your right hand holds me secure. If I say 'surely this darkness will drown me' even the night will glow with Your light around me.

Psalm 139: 4 & 9-11 ARIA

Rain / Reign

Healing rain has come before
    and is coming again.

Today, I trust You Lord
    and know You're coming back again.

You reign in the heavens
    and here on earth.

Your rain is refreshing
    for my soul –
        healing
            as I open my heart wide
                as I open my eyes to Your rain.

They shall fear Thee as
long as the sun and moon
endure, throughout all
generations.

He shall come down like rain upon the mown
grass: as showers that water the earth.

In his days shall the righteous flourish;
and abundance of peace so long as the moon
endureth.

Psalm 72 5-7 KJV

Let us draw near with a true heart in full assurance of faith, having our hearts sprinkled from an evil conscience, and our bodies washed with pure water.

Hebrews 10:22 KJV

Trusting

My soul is weary

    it's been a long battle

I see a light

    at the end of the tunnel.

        Not there yet.

        God, shall I continue

            to trust in You

                that you'll bring me through?

Gone

Please Lord help us to heal...

    heal from the heartbreak

When a loved one

    who's no longer there...

        now a silhouette memory,

Oh, how You care.

Can we see?

    Not really, yet...

        Only to imagine

    open arms in greeting

        at a reunification in heaven.

    Gone, but not gone.

Joy Full

Joy comes in the morning

    to light a warm fire within

        a delight on the inside,

            sorrow departs

Joy speaks of heaven

    of things to come,

of worship continually and

    feeling spiritually full to the brim.

Revival

Oh, Lord,

I come to You in prayer

to ponder and muse...

What will revival

look like

when You

bring breakthrough?!

By

By the calm waters

    is where You lead,

        to rest, rejuvenate

and to take heed.

Blessed is the devoted one who doesn't choose to walk in the counsel of the wicked. Nor do they walk staunchly in the ways of sinners, nor inhabits the dwelling places of mockers.

By the calm waters

    are our prayers presented,

Instead, their delight is in following the instruction of

        whispers, loud shouts

the Lord. And in God's directions they mediate and

    crying out for a mending of hearts affected

ponder out loud all day and night.

By the calm waters

    is where we can come

        Come to bring our pain, sorrow, joys,

    and dream of things to come.

They are like a tree that's planted and rooted deeply by the rivers of water,

By the calm waters

    is where we can head

bringing forth it's fruit in the right season, and whose leaves doesn't wither.

        to be refreshed,

All they do will prosper in the Lord.

    feel light and protected.

Psalm 1: 1-3 ACTA

Bottled Tears

Dear God,

Today a tear slips down my cheek.

    A tear of joy.

It lands in my palm

    much to my delight

I'm thankful for tears that are not always

    birthed from pain.

The tears from another yesterday

    sting in my memory,

    but Your restoration flowed in

like gold set in broken vases,

    like healing liquid now set in the new,

    with Your cross as the shield of victory.

You bottle our tears

    as One holding precious our cares.

Thank you, Lord, for caring,

>You're such a mighty

and wonderful God.

I'm forever grateful,

>grateful to You.

Warm Arms

Dearest God, wonderful loving Father,

Counselor, our Prince of Peace.

    May You wrap Your arms around

    anyone hurting today.

That they would know Your love

        And the words of comfort You want to say.

Cast your worries upon the Lord, and He'll sustain and take care of you. He won't ever allow the righteous to be shaken.

Psalm 55:22 ARTA

In All

Lord God,

my heart is in wonder that You're in all

In the summer sun

in the dark of the night

in the opening of petals in Spring

in the thundering of the ocean waves

in the delicacy of a floating snowflake

in the flowing of hot magma under the earth

in our hearts with love and compassion

in the roaring of Your lion's heart to protect us

in all.

Victory

Oh Jesus,
    Today's the day for a prayer of victory,
        one that says thank You and that
            You hold the victory.
Nothing can shake us
    no weapon formed,
        those rattling keys You took from
        the depths
            now held in victory.
Your position on the cross of love,
    that day that the enemy was doomed.
You're the rider on the white horse,
    carrying a banner
    A name is on Your forehead
    and nothing else will matter.

In the beginning

                          in the end

      in the midst

You are Almighty

    and I'm declaring

        Your victory!

Don't fear, says the Lord who created you,
O Jacob, and He who formed you, O Israel.

For I have redeemed your life, I have called
you by your name - you are Mine.

When you pass through turbulent waters,
I am with you.
And when you wade through strong-flowing
rivers, they will not overwhelm you.

When you walk through the fire, you will
not be burnt, nor will the flames scorch you.

For, I am the Lord your God, the Holy
One of Israel, your Saviour.

Isaiah 43:16-3a ARIA

Hope

'Oh little one,

so precious to Me,

Hope is coming

Hope is uncovering

the darkness;

a shimmering light.

Hope is from Me,

a beam of light

that warmth remains.'

~ love from God.

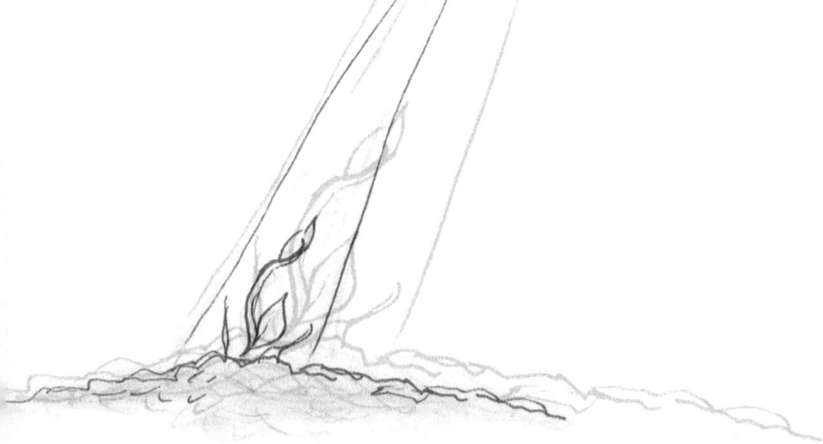

Look Up

Looking up, I see a smile.
    I know it's a sign.
        That God's smiling at me.

  A shape in a cloud to some,
      but to me
          a promise to come…

Oh barren land, it's no obstacle to You
    but instead, opportunities for streams in the desert.
    fires in hearts
    quenched by living waters from the sky.

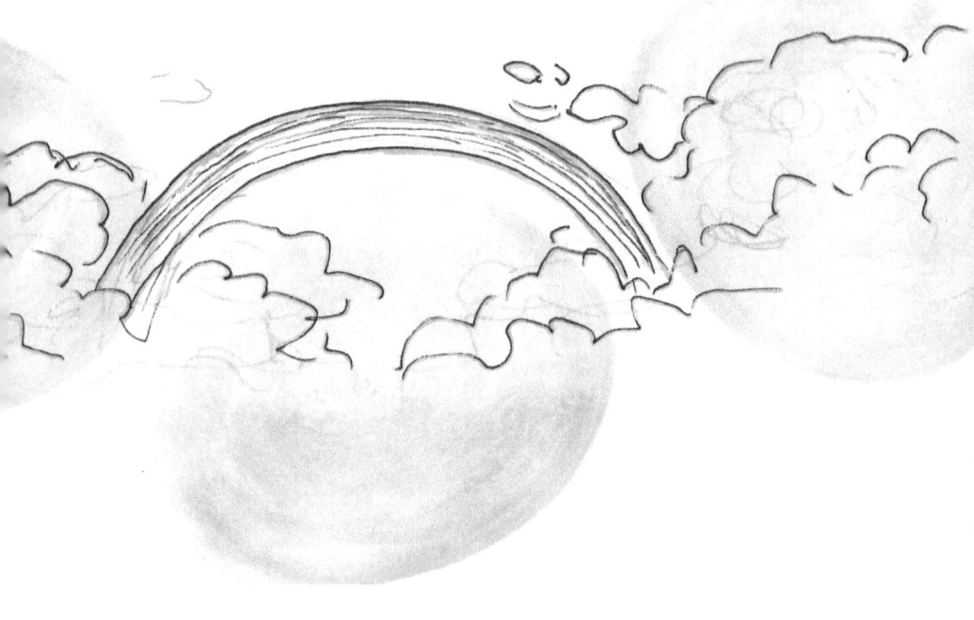

A sign,
    a whisper.
        a knowing smile
            of things to come.

Free

'Not to worry

    My dear one,'

        I hear You say.

There's a treasure that's hidden,

        but not.

In Your Word

    shines a light

To know that there's not a day

    we need to worry about.

        And to hold onto You

    with all our might.

Therefore I say unto you, Take no thought for your life, what ye shall eat, or what ye shall drink; nor yet for your body, what ye shall put on. Is not the life more than meat, and the body than raiment?

Behold the fowls of the air: for they sow not, neither do they reap, nor gather into barns; yet your heavenly Father feedeth them. Are ye not much better than they?

Which of you by taking thought can add one cubit unto his stature?

And why take ye thought for raiment? Consider the lilies of the field, how they grow; they toil not, neither do they spin:

And yet I say unto you, That even Solomon in all his glory was not arrayed like one of these.

Wherefore, if God so clothe the grass of the field, which to day is, and to morrow is cast into the oven, shall he not much more clothe you, O ye of little faith?

Therefore take no thought, saying, What shall we eat? or, What shall we drink? or, Wherewithal shall we be clothed?

(For after all these things do the Gentiles seek:) for your heavenly Father knoweth that ye have need of all these things.

But seek ye first the kingdom of God, and his righteousness; and all these things shall be added unto you.

Take therefore no thought for the morrow: for the morrow shall take thought for the things of itself. Sufficient unto the day is the evil thereof.

Matthew 6:25-34 KJV

Light

Dear Lord,

    Oh, Maker of Heaven and Earth,

        Heavenly realms and an

           earthly footstool.

Please send Your light

    that pierces the darkness,

        Your light that heals,

           uncovers truths,

           shows the way

           guides with light.

Praise

Lord Jesus,

Today I pray these prayer requests

    will soon turn into praise moments

As we see You move unshakeable mountains

    flexing Your arms for all to see.

To see, praise, have joy

    and celebrate all You've done.

Dance of Life

Oh Lord,

May I dance the rest

    of the Way throughout life?

Dance with You

    Dance like never before

Leaping high

    twirling about

        stretching out

            and smiling with one accord

Falling in love

    with each flow of hand,

        here and now,

           gracefully moving around

knowing how deep,

           how wide,

Your love unconditional

                         that never runs out.

> O the depth of the riches both of the wisdom and knowledge of God!
>
> Romans 11: 33a KJV

Shining

I feel desperate for understanding today, God

    where can I find Your truths?

all that glitters isn't seeming like gold…

But Your Word –

    a treasure beyond measure

has the real sparkle

    as You lift that treasure box lid

        we find wisdom.

It has depths that are endless

    and provisions abounding

a revealing – love unconditional

    and of things to come.

Knowing
the Unseen Realm

To know is to see You

    to see what You open

        another everything exists

    beyond our wildest imagination

    there, a glimpse,

        something I've never seen before

      now seeing

Something that can never be unseen in my heart

and now forever more

something that's more than known from You.

Come to Me, all those who are heavy-hearted and burdened by life's troubles – I will give you true rest.

            Matthew 11:28 ARIA

Light and Free

Free,

light

what does this feel like?

Free,

light

Is it beyond reach,

in my wildest dreams?

I'm thankful to know You

and know now that You have already

paid the price

on the cross for our freedom

So we can live

free,

light.

Like Honey

God, is Your love like honey

    I ponder

Sweet, attractive, good

    nourishing like

        unconditional love,

gold in liquid

    dripping everywhere

not ceasing

    unconditionally remaining

healthy to digest, runs afar

sticks to our hearts, our souls and minds,

A love that never goes off for those that draw near

    renewing afresh,

    in Your love we never need to fear.

Transcending

What does time look like
> when time is endless,
>> when doors are never closed
>>> when eternity is ever fathomed?

How can we know what yet exists?
> Yet a glimpse given
>> in Your Word sets us apart

Reaching
> loving
>> living life,
>>> revelations
>>>> Free to wonder.

Delight

My heart is heavy,

    but Your Word stands strong

In one moment,

    a twinkling of the eye

        everything can change.

In Your presence,

    suddenly…

Light,

    free,

        in peace

In Your hands,

      forever

To be continued....

MORE BOOKS ARE COMING SOON IN

THE *Grace Lane Poetry* COLLECTION:

Hope Renewing

Hope Everlasting

Kataleya loves being near calm ocean waters, where she spends time with God, feeling inspired by His wonderful creation and what He puts on her heart to write.

She also pens letters for Grace Lane, a newsletter featuring beautiful ocean and nature photography alongside scripture and encouraging thoughts about God's grace, love and hope.

Find more at

gracelane.substack.com

www.ingramcontent.com/pod-product-compliance
Lightning Source LLC
LaVergne TN
LVHW090038080526
838202LV00046B/3864